W9-ACR-396

Cherry Pickers

BY HAL ROGERS

Published by The Child's World®
1980 Lookout Drive • Mankato, MN 56003-1705
800-599-READ • www.childsworld.com

Acknowledgments
The Child's World®: Mary Berendes, Publishing Director
The Design Lab: Design
Jody Jensen Shaffer: Editing
Pamela J. Mitsakos: Photo Research

Photos
All-Kind-ZA Photography/iStock.com: 19; cjp/iStock.com: 12; David M. Budd Photography: 15; dlewis33/iStock.com: 20; gmattrichard/iStock.com: cover, 1; gpflman/iStock.com: 7; Kratka Photography/iStock.com: 11; Simply Creative Photography/iStock.com: 16; Steven Frame/iStock.com: 8; Kondrachov Vladimir/Shutterstock.com: 4

ISBN 9781623239633
LCCN 2013947249

Printed in the United States of America
Mankato, MN
September, 2014
PA02249

Contents

These workers are using a cherry picker to get close to power lines.

4

What is a cherry picker?

A cherry picker is a special machine. It has a long arm. The arm lifts workers high. Ladders can reach some high places. But cherry pickers can reach even more.

What are the parts of a cherry picker?

Many cherry pickers sit on the back of a truck. The truck has a **cab**. The driver sits in the cab. The driver moves the truck where it needs to go.

cab

boom

bucket

8

The back of the truck is flat. The long arm sits on top. The arm is called a **boom**. The end of the boom has a **bucket**. A worker can stand in the bucket.

The boom lifts the bucket high. It moves the bucket from side to side. It moves the bucket forward and backward. It puts the worker in just the right spot.

This worker is cutting branches from a tree.

STOP

95 dB

This worker is using the outside controls to move the boom.

How do you steer a cherry picker?

There are **controls** in the bucket. There are controls on the outside of the truck, too. The controls make the arm go up and down. They make it turn from side to side. Workers use the controls to move to the right place.

Do cherry pickers tip over?

The boom goes so high! You would think the cherry picker would tip over. But it has heavy stands called **outriggers**. The workers put down the outriggers. The outriggers hold the cherry picker still. They keep it from tipping over.

The outriggers are made of heavy metal.

This worker is fixing a light over a parking lot.

How are cherry pickers used?

Cherry pickers are used for many jobs. They help workers reach phone and cable lines. They help people pick fruit from tall trees. They help people cut high tree branches. They help them change lightbulbs on tall streetlights.

Cherry pickers help workers reach power lines, too. Power lines carry **electricity**. The electricity can hurt or kill people. Workers must be very careful around power lines.

This worker is using a cherry picker to get close to a power line.

19

Sometimes lots of cherry pickers are used for one job.

Are cherry pickers important?

Cherry pickers are very important. They help workers stay safe in high places. They help them do their jobs. Try watching for cherry pickers. You will see them doing many jobs!

GLOSSARY

boom (BOOM) A boom is a long arm that holds something up.

bucket (BUK-et) A cherry picker's bucket is a basket where the worker stands.

cab (KAB) A machine's cab is the area where the driver sits.

controls (kun-TROHLZ) Controls are parts that people use to run a machine.

electricity (ee-lek-TRI-si-tee) Electricity is a kind of power or energy. It is used for heat and light and to make things move.

outriggers (OWT-rih-gurz) Outriggers are strong stands that keep some machines from tipping.

BOOKS

Barkan, Joanne, and Richard Walz (illustrator). *Big Wheels*. Mahwah, NJ: Whistlestop/Troll, 1996.

Hoban, Tana. *Construction Zone*. New York: Greenvillow Books, 1997.

Sturges, Philemon, and Shari Halpern (illustrator). *I Love Trucks!* New York: HarperCollins, 1999.

Zobel, Derek. *Bucket Trucks*. Minneapolis, MN: Bellwether Media, 2009.

WEB SITES

Visit our Web site for lots of links about cherry pickers: **childsworld.com/links**

Note to parents, teachers, and librarians: We routinely check our Web links to make sure they're safe, active sites—so encourage your readers to check them out!

INDEX

ABOUT THE AUTHOR

Hal Rogers has written over a dozen books on machines and trucks. A longtime resident of Colorado, Hal currently lives in Denver, along with his family, a fuzzy cat named Simon, and a lovable dog named Sebastian.